Witold Lutoslawski

GRAVE

for cello and piano

CHESTER MUSIC

This work was first performed on 22nd April 1981 by Roman Jablonski (cello) and Krystyna Borucinska (piano), in the hall of the National Museum, Warsaw.

in memoriam Stefan Jarociński

GRAVE

METAMORPHOSES FOR 'CELLO AND PIANO

Witold Lutoslawski
1981

in memoriam Stefan Jarociński

GRAVE
METAMORPHOSES FOR 'CELLO AND PIANO

Witold Lutoslawski
1981